A GOD LOVING ATHEIST

Marta O'Conner-Suarez

A GOD LOVING

ATHEIST

Marta O'Conner-Suarez

A God Loving Atheist
Copyright © 2012 by Marta O'Conner-Suarez
www.manufacturingobjectives.com

ISBN 978-0-9853062-0-5

Printed in USA by 48HrBooks (www.48HrBooks.com)

Dedication

This book is dedicated to my children Rayshawn O'Conner, Shadow O'Conner, and Jada Mason. The chapters to follow will forever be my everlasting word for your years to come. To James (JT) Mason for showing me that love is possible.

Also to the following people because regardless you serve as a big part of my life: Vilma Suarez, Charol Conner, Evette Fernandez, the O'Conner-Suarez and Mason Family, and to the Marines who I had a pleasure of serving with.

With Much love,

        Marta O'Conner-Suarez

Preface

The words that fill these pages have seen trials in actions and today serve as a living testimony. It is both a guide and a story and I hope as the writer that I accomplish self recognition within the reader. Take from these pages a sense of yourself as you embark upon pages of my experiences.

This book is marked by obstacles and a journey far from over. The pages contained within have been written for those willing and daring to give insight a chance. You have taken the first step in walking in my shoes and putting life back into my past. Step into years of footprints that are now only an arm's reach away.

Come and follow me through time. Having the opportunity to share my story with you is beyond remarkable. It is a "one in a million" chance that I take great pleasure in sharing with you. It means even more to know that this book will start as a story and end as a memory that will forever live.

My story is marked in stone but has become an impact because of you.....the reader. I have recorded into history my personal life for others to experience. Therefore, I hope to take you by the hand and assist your mind to open up to a different view.

I began writing these chapters with enthusiasm and hopes of putting a permanent mark for my children. Giving them my history, experience, and endeavors finely annotated and available with the turn of a page. I thank you again for making that goal possible.

Go ahead now, turn the pages of time and keep my story alive.......

Table of Contents

CHAPTER ONE: MIRROR IMAGE

This story began to unfold in the image of hate, anger, and loneliness. At a very young age I had experienced what it was like to give up hope and solely rely on obstacles but not so much believing that trust and love were remotely possible. By The age of 10 I was fully aware of my environment and the "Impossible", as I would always label my circumstances. I eventually started to feel as though my only chance at life was to avoid it all together by not accepting that a chain of bad events could be changed.

It was like staring in the mirror and only seeing through despair eyes the image of the body while lacking the sense of the soul. I was staring my own life in the eyes and yet I had not summoned the strength to break through the hateful chain. My family was poor in resources and advantages in life but even more in faith. We had spent our entire childhood learning the ways of the "STREET" hoping that it would set us in the right direction because there was nothing more important than to "....demand respect". We had given our family a foundation that over the years would not be able to hold firm. By the age of 14 my family had already drifted so far apart that we had struggle at simple conversations.

It was at this same age that I strongly believed that nothing was going to be made positive.....at least not for this family, not for my brothers, not for my sisters, and especially not for me. Instead of trying to change the common characteristics I decided that it was best suited to accept and adapt. I left behind any hope of success and fell in the loneliness of my environment. I knew that my family felt the same because I could see beyond the silence. Even through the arguments that they would have I could see the desire in their eyes to just say "I Love You". But that, in our family, would only be a sign of weakness.

I couldn't quite understand why we were so unfortunate to belong to a family that was far from the norm. I couldn't see how my peers at school could have so much support in their athletic abilities and educational achievements. I couldn't believe that a family could sit down at a dinner table and be thankful. Most importantly I couldn't see where GOD was!!!

At this phase God had been just a name, a hopeless excuse for others to feel fulfilled. God had become my enemy, one who I could not confront and it only angered me more not to be able to ask the "Why?." I had felt like he needed to explain so much to me but where is he? Where could I find this great person who forgot about me, about my family, and about our suffering? I had felt like a fool for once believing he would find me lost in the pile of tears but my wait became longer than the answers. So I had given up hope.

My days were marked with that constant reminder that I was far from a blessing and even more from a miracle because God had forgotten me. I couldn't sit back and keep convincing myself into poorly concluded hypothesis that God would be there. So I began to carry myself as such, I pronounced myself an ATHEIST. I refused God's existence as I felt mine had been. I was purposely at war with God...this time I didn't care about getting the "Why?" because I had my "Why not!"

There was no better feeling for me than to feel like I had stood to the fight. I wasn't sure of my purpose in life but I strongly felt that it definitely had nothing to do with "God" himself. This was a world on its own and if heaven existed then I had become a victim of it in many ways. It had become my mission to express loudly to others my own experience so that they too could see that nothing was through God but by coincidence.

No human being could convince me that I was wrong because they too were a being. What sense would it make for me to believe the suppose facts from someone else who couldn't explain to me how I had become the bad apple in the bunch. An individual who couldn't tell me why God couldn't stand up to me himself and show me he was there. It had no sense at all.

So there I was, hateful, angry and lonely because of this so-called "GOD". Ironically it had been the same foundation that filled my entire childhood and developed into my young adult hood. Amazingly, I could still see that hopeless image immerge from the past to only remind me that nothing had changed for me as far as I could see. It proved that only one thing could remain constant---that God had been a poorly executed methodology.

I disliked the sight of church-goers and pastors who would preach the word of an unknown character. You couldn't see God, touch God or hear God so why throw hope into someone else's path! It was like trying to hit the Jack Pot with a set of numbers you had always believed were your personally significant ones. It was like those Christmas days when our parents warned us that negative behavior would put us on Santa's naughty list. Only to find out over the years that Santa Clause had been an exaggerated story to convince us to believe in it. The crazy part was that once we placed our faith into the idea it was then that we would find out that it was just a "small white lie".

Well I wasn't going to let myself be driven by another technique that would only become another small white lie. It had become a reality for me to be against the world and fend for myself. I had been subjected to enough and now I was prepared to live life. Of course, live life in my own understanding. I was my own guidance and believer and if I was going to make it through the years ahead then I had to leave behind those childhood parables that proved nothing.

I was determined, I was dedicated, I was prepared ...but I was lonely. Lonely indeed, it was one of the most confusing feelings in the world. To be around your family but not have a family around. To have a talent and no one to see it. To achieve so much academically and no one to notice. To be at the top but still feel like you're at the bottom.

I could see the same in my mother and siblings, the same exact feeling but I didn't know how to reach out and close that gap. Neither how to be that support system in order to break that chain. We just ignored the facts and carried ourselves as though no burden was weighing heavily. We had become our own prosecutors without evidence. It was just much easier to pretend our sorrows didn't exist. Plus "God" had not been there before so what was the difference now?

My mother had made attempts at bringing God into the equation but it felt like she picked her moments when it would best fit her needs. It only helped me conclude that it was just all a joke. That she may have believed only because all else worked in her odds so it would only be reasonable to lean on the something equivalent to the unforeseen obstacles---an unseen leader. She was true in her understanding, it was apparent but it had yet to show the growing plant of her sowed seed.

11

I've tried on occasion to seek the path and see if God would finally take up the fight with me and just say "Here I am". I know I was setting a test with no answers but every time I made attempts at seeking God it felt like another step back. It was already difficult trying to find the proof to his existence. I had actually hoped to be proven wrong because it was not important for me to be right. I had wanted to be the pawn in a chess game that was overtaken by the king but instead it always ended at "Check-mate".

Either God didn't find it reason enough to give me a sign or I was becoming more naive with time. It was really difficult to be at a constant struggle with trying to find that solid foundation. Due to the lack of the family bond it had become obvious that I wanted God to show his existence to me so that I could feel someone cared. That reassurance couldn't be possible by just finding a church home because I desired the privacy of my own feelings. I had learned over the years to show little or no emotion. Now here I was stuck between reality and the supernatural.

I could clearly remember times when our family would gather together and somehow, without warning, there would be a dispute. It had never failed. It was as though, no matter what, we had to pick sides in our family because no occasion went in peace. I couldn't stand the sight but what more could I do? The fact was I didn't have the strength to go against the odds. Not because I didn't want to at one point or another but it seemed easier to just sit back and let "bygones be bygones".

It had seemed like the perfect solution to our growing problem at the time. We had been so resistant towards each other for so many years that it had become second nature. The sad part was that we were safer with strangers than with each other. I know that they too felt the same. It became clearer when at the age of 17 I had moved into the home of a complete stranger. I was attending College in Chicago (Robert Morris College) and had refused to communicate with my family members.

There I was in College, first in the immediate family, with no support, no money and yet at a strangers home for shelter. Seldom did my family ask about me or me for them. There seemed to be a level of satisfaction in our actions but that feeling soon proved to be a heart ache. Years later, after my schooling had been completed, I had decided to join the Marine Corps. It was with the intent of just getting away from what I thought was everything.

On September 25, 2005, I had set foot in Parris Island, South Carolina on the "Yellow Foot Prints" which served as every recruit's stepping stone into the Marine Corps. I remember being yelled at and rushed to complete necessary tasks but all I could think about was "This is better than home". I immediately became anxious to complete my three months of training. I wanted to prove to myself that I could make it past the odds without my family. But yet again I had been wrong.....

November 23rd, 2005, I had graduated from boot camp, it had brought me to tears for two reason; I had earned my title as a United States Marine, and I didn't have the support of my family there. Just a friend and older brother who would serve as my transportation back home. It had been then that I had cursed God. How could I have stood out in High School, College, Running, and now in the Marine Corps and he still couldn't bless me with a family that could come together. How could there be a God if there had been no justice for my desire to carry the family name in a positive nature?

The Marine Corps had made me a different person already; it had thought me the discipline to make quick and reasonable decisions under stressful situations. It emphasized the importance of sticking together as a family. In the same perspective, I wanted to carry this home to my biological family but it began to feel unrealistic. At this point in my life we were more like strangers. Therefore I maintained my distance to avoid the heartache. Eventually I was somehow now at war with both my family and God.

CHAPTER TWO: PREPARING FOR WAR

By the age of 20 I was packing my bags and preparing to experience my first deployment. I had arrived in Al-Asad, Iraq on January 11, 2007. I was fully aware of the purpose we had there and that mission came first. Although the Marine Corps infantry and other branches of services had worked jointly to keep combat neutral and a minimal impact to the Logistic side, I still had to keep a combat sense. I had to be on the alert, not as much as our elite infantry who I considered the "Guardian Angels" of Aviation but enough to be prepared to respond.

Three months into my deployment I started to feel like a grieving widow. I was becoming emotionally burdened by the past history of my family and I didn't know if I should lean on them for closure. I was away from two young children, newlywed by less than a year, and now I was still counting over 300 days before my return. I made a family of my peers and my superiors. Even with that I felt a gap in my life. I needed my biological family.

It was truly important at this point to see my family come together so I could have reassurance that my children would be properly cared for. It was no longer about me, now I was struggling with leaving behind a foundation for my kids. The stress was piling on but I didn't have many resources that would serve me any purpose. Instead I sought God. Yes! The one symbol I had refused thus far. I was still in doubt but I placed my stress into my hands for God to hear.

I'm not sure if God answered but months started to feel like mere days. Somehow I had forgotten all about the stressors in my life and had been able to function in the right state of mind. There was a phase of peace for me and for the first time in my life I was able to cope.

I made very few attempts at seeking God since then because I wasn't fully convinced in miracles or blessings. I knew that in my heart I was nothing more than an Atheist. Clearly defined by its definition of a non-believer. So I had to start making a solid choice for myself, will I seek God or avoid him all together?

Well to my own surprise I had decided mid way through my deployment that hate had led me into some stressful situations. It couldn't hurt to give God a chance regardless of how I felt. I started to analyze my understanding of God. I went back to my comparison of God to Santa Clause and figured "What could be so bad in a child receiving a reward for not making it to Santa's naughty list". Yes, we may have been slightly deceived but in the end there was satisfaction for both parties.

So that was me "the child" and God was "the father". Whether he was fooling me or not the conclusion could not possibly fall short of satisfaction. I was willing, at this point, to accept a "little white lie" because I was seeking a reward. It was a challenge but how many times have I been in fear when a challenge presented itself and with a bit of effort overcame that fear---plenty. What can I lose from believing faithfully in something that could only make me positive in mind?! NOTHING.

On December 22, 2007 my tour in Al-Asad, Iraq was completed and I was received by my then husband. My mother and siblings were nowhere in sight for my arrival but that didn't bother me anymore. I understood that they too were struggling with the same and it was a chain we had stretched too far between one another. I had finally made it through one war and was now preparing to battle another because I still desired my family's bond.

There had been this overwhelming feeling deep down for my family's happiness. I wanted to be proud of them and them of me. I prayed for them in hopes that it would change things. In the hardest parts of time I found that it wasn't enough. I was starting to have my marital issues most of which involved church. It was as though I had given myself to God and he had decided to take my relationship as repayment.

My husband was attending church as a musician both for himself and the money but somewhere along that line I felt that I wasn't considered. I knew this wasn't a fact but we weren't on the same level of faith just yet. It angered me some because I felt we spoke two different spiritual languages. Here he was cleansing his soul while I couldn't understand two cents of what the church was speaking.

I stopped going all together. I couldn't possibly be a support system while confused in my own understanding. I heard a pastor once say **"A family that prays together stays together"**. I thought, "Well how can one know how to pray without a teacher". It was as though I was expected to know God by now. Well fact was---I didn't. I needed someone to take me under their wings. Sort of like a helpless newborn needing assistance being fed and clothed.

The confusion was so over bearing that I decided once again that God was working against me. I went from one war to another on an indefinite basis. Right when I had decided to give God a chance into my life he had drifted my marriage away. I blamed God because the results were heading in a direction against my devotion to change. How can I comprehend being the bad apple again! I was setting myself for God and now my husband and I couldn't understand one another.

I could remember clearly how our arguments would about me not wanting God in my life therefore pushing him from God. That may have sounded like a perfectly put conclusion but in my eyes it wasn't that way. My morals on marriage were equivalent to that mentioned in the bible of husband and wife. I wasn't afraid neither to give in nor to love. The odd factor was that I wasn't willing to speak a different spiritual language and be left behind to figure it out alone.

In marriage, I strongly believed in partnership. Well, that was what I required in this journey---a partner. I tried to understand my husband but somehow always failed. This included being misunderstood on my own purposes with faith. So I finally took my arguments to God. I let God have it his way by allowing myself not to be in the way of my husband and his church. It wasn't the best of my decisions though.

By the third year in our marriage I had grown so much in hate again that now my husband had become my enemy. The more he would try and bring God into the equation the more my barriers grew. I was building my walls between the two of us with hate. I was fully aware of my hateful nature at this point but it seemed fit. It was the solution to being left alone in the spiritual world where I had already been alone in the physical one. It was a 'lose-lose' environment for me.

I had been so accustomed to losing that I didn't give interest in winning. Especially not this battle because winning meant God would be in the picture again. The one who I had considered the factor in my relationship reaching turmoil. We didn't fight about the same factors most relationships did, we fought about the level of each other's faith. How God was in one and one was in God but what to do with the other---me!

What was it about me that just couldn't maintain a straight and narrowed path? On countless occasions it seemed like every corner I turned there appeared another. I couldn't necessarily see where to go because it was just that complicating of a path.

I didn't feel like a victim but a target. I knew enough about myself to see that I wasn't a terrible person. I maintained a very open and giving heart towards others. I did not desire luxury at all. I had feared that the cost of wanting material things would be losing it. I didn't expect anything from anyone nor weighted my stress on someone else's shoulders.

On the flipped side, it seemed like the world wanted a lot from me. It had been determined to take everything in my life and make it negative. There was no avoiding its transformation. It had me marked and I couldn't change that. I was left with no resources to pull myself back together. I was fighting back but it had already conquered my family, my attempt at faith, and now my marriage.

CHAPTER THREE: UNCONDITIONAL LOVE

Love needed to play its role into my life. Somehow I needed to understand for myself that obstacles are meant to be conquered. I needed to fight back and not allow them to surrender me into the lonely world I had settled with. It was my responsibility, as much as everyone else's, to become humbled in our ways.

I needed to find the strength to love unconditionally. This was required if I was going to make progression with my family and my husband. The problem was; where was I going to get the strength from? I needed for everything to make a turn for the better.

Seeking God was still a fluctuation in this equation because I had yet to stop the blame. Plus, it wasn't necessary for me to do this with God. Like any other part of my life, I wanted to prove myself with what little I've received from the world. I was sure I could love unconditionally without putting faith in God but instead put effort in my desire.

There had been a clear understanding within myself that God couldn't help me through this phase. He couldn't possibly be of any help in me learning to love unconditionally. He was once the reason I felt excused for a hateful perspective. So I had my reserved opinion on his potential in this matter.

Sure enough I had found myself making effort in understanding my own life. I shared neutral feelings with my mom and siblings from time to time. It was definitely more constant than I had years ago. I could hear in their voice how grateful they were being able to see eye to eye for once. We began to turn the silence in our hearts into words of actions.

Finally, we were communicating and treating the open wound. Even if it left a scar, we were sure it would be healed from the pain. All along we have all wanted the same---a family bond. It was relieving to know that I wasn't so alone in the feeling. We had, for the first time, found a common ground where to relate these emotions.

It help relieved some of my concerns for my children. I had always feared the same separation occurring with them and the rest of the family. I didn't want this to curse generations after us. Our children didn't need to walk in our shoes. Those shoes wear worn out with ego and hatred.

The only thing left for us to do was to come together as a family in one place. We needed to prove to one another that we could sit down as a family and remain humbled. To see love and not seek a foe among each other. Now I needed to find how to accomplish this. I had made it this far with my family, though baby steps, and didn't want them to start losing focus.

My husband on the other hand needed my support. He needed to see that I could love him unconditionally and vice-versa. We had one big difference to work out----God. Though I had kept my reservation I needed to accept that his work was defined differently. Therefore, I accepted his desire with the church but seldom did I ask about his experience.

He also accepted that my path did not cross with his dedication. We were two strangers in one relationship but that was fine with us. We had many unspoken words of a bigger part of ourselves but yet we stood firm. That served as a turning point for me because at least now we had accepted the differences. There was just one major hill to climb- how long will we be separated by belief?

Now here I was with two major obstacles in my way. On one hand I had my family needing to come together in love and on the other I had my marriage that needed closure. I had assumed these tasks with the hope of seeing it through all the way. I was not quitting but these were two obstacles that required more than just me. My family had already made as much progression as they could and my marriage had met the end of the resolution. Neither one had made it far enough though, not to my satisfaction.

Naturally, someone would reach out and tell me to seek God. Well I did not. Instead, I let time play its wild card. I didn't interfere with time so that it may show its lesson. I figured if we could see how bad things are for ourselves then eventually understanding could be made possible.

The idea didn't work to a full effect. Time had only allowed us to lean in our own understanding of the situations we were faced with. With no communication we had allowed more room for the finger pointing. This had only led back to hate and discontent. We were back to step one. I was disappointed but somehow I wasn't surprise that this could occur. To me, this was our norm and I could see how change could prove impossible. How could I have expected time to work solely without effort?

What I had failed to see was that I needed to show them evidence of the possibility rather than allow them to lean back into the old ways. It felt like I wasn't going to accomplish much in these personal matters in my life. It was frustration after frustration from that point. I, at least, wanted these factors to work themselves into good outcomes.

It was a hopeless reality for me at such a point in my life. If no one could support the way for these situations then it would fall further unto the waist side. Without a shadow of doubt, I knew I would feel liable for the consequences of this failure. Although it wasn't solely my responsibility it had been a desired goal. It took so much effort just to accomplish baby steps and now it took nothing to bring everything to a halt. Just like that it all fell into pieces!

CHAPTER FOUR: A SIGHT TO SEE

The site of reality was soon to approach. It was not long before I would have to visit my husband's family. I was filled with concern because I knew what our differences were. I understood that our individual environments had an impact on our ways.

I had expected to see a group of people cluster in one corner prepared to stop a fight or an altercation. I was estimating that by the end of our trip we would be talking about the rumors and some of the constant negative behaviors associated with the family. I assumed obvious poor decisions would be lurking in this visit. Most of all, I figured every other word in the conversations would include a curse word here and there.

Apparently, I had underestimated this visit and this family. Upon arrival I was greeted by his mother, who by the looks, seemed like a humbled person by nature. I followed them into the home and continue to observe this now strange environment. I must admit that I had felt almost shy around them. They were actually happy to see one another.

The conversations were mostly about church and music. They would talk on these topics for hours. I couldn't understand how this could be possible. How could they be so comfortable with each other? Of course, everything was not positive for them but one thing was clear- they had a bond. That bond was God.

They seemed at least satisfied with life as a family regardless of the stones life threw at them. I was in awe and realized at this moment that God had not failed me, I had failed God. I had been seeking him for my own desire and not his purpose for me. This reality felt like a torment to my very soul. I was convinced through my own sight that anything was possible through God.

I had hated God for my upbringing, my struggle, and the loneliness I had endured. All this time had passed in my life and yet God was seasonal for me. I just wanted to cry out loud but it wasn't the right place. I started to look back at my own life where I had assume God had never been there for me and with just a little faith I SAW GOD!

God had given me life at birth when my chances were slim to none, God had set me aside from the trend that held others behind, God had given me a scholarship when I had not sought one, God had put me through College, God had guided me in the Marine Corps, God had kept me alive in my deployment, God had even put me in a position to be able to pull my family through.....God never forgot about me.

Finding God was like finding a needle in a haystack. He definitely had a purpose for me that I wanted to hear. I began to read the bible for more understanding. It was then that I learn to "walk by faith and not by sight". If I was going to hear God speak to me then I would have to open my heart for him to reach me.

The more I read the bible the more my burden fell to my chest. I felt like the devil's prey. I had allowed all the ways of the flesh to confuse the ability of the soul. I just wanted to drop at God's mercy. He had turned my life around in a simple visit. This was too much for me to share with my husband so I still remained silent of my own transformation. So while my husband went to church assuming we were still at the halt in our belief I was home reading the bible and having my talk with God.

God's love was much greater than I had estimated. All this time and he had still loved me enough to work constantly in putting me on the right track. When I would curse him and deny him he would only forgive me. He wasn't tearing my marriage apart, he was trying to put us in one narrowed path but I pushed against the grain. I was still skeptical of my full devotion to God because I didn't want to be consumed so quickly into change. I had then questioned whether going to church was positive for me or not.

This was critical because now I had to decide how far to carry my faith. I had learned enough about God at this point to know that I needed to be "born again". This required my attendance in a church of my wanting and my pledge to God himself. It sounded a bit unrealistic for me but I was sure that faith involved trust. So I trusted.

I began attending church on rare terms. Moving fast on this transformation wasn't a leading project. I wanted to see for myself the true nature of these "church goers" and see for myself how positive this change would prove. Also, I had read the bible but wasn't knowledgeable in finding verses. I was not capable of finding a verse if you told me the page number. So I decided to slow my pace on the church attendance until I could feel more comfortable adapting to the environment.

Funny thing was that I became more excited to learn more about God once I had educated myself with the basic concepts. My understanding stood at a neutral level now. I could finally comprehend the morals of the preaching's and the songs. It felt wonderful to finally feel so filtered from hate.

In comparison, it was like going to counseling. It was like taking a seat on a comfortable couch and nearby stood a stranger with a look of care. He was a stranger who couldn't wait to hear all your troubles regardless of the situation. Time may have been limited in a sense but yet that was all the time required for the moment. This stranger then would make a personal file of your troubles until your next visit. This file would later be an old portrait of one's hardship and serve as evidence of our trials.

This is how I felt about God now, I was comfortable in this room with him and we could talk all my problems away. By the end of my visit I would feel whole again. If a time came for me to need a lift all I had to do was come back and he could pull my file out. Eventually, we would both sit back and laugh at this old portrait and I would probably say, with a smile, "Where did you find this old picture?"

I'm almost sure to God it may have been like finding that lost child that had wondered off. Too young to defend herself from the dangers and not wise enough to find the way home. I was the one whom everyone had giving up the hope of finding alive because it was a hope far from reach. God, on the other hand didn't give up the search. Of course, a parent's instinct out weight the average conclusion. I was sure he had made that stressful search alone hoping that I had not given up being found. He was on a constant move at finding that trail I left behind with my grievance.

As imaginary as this may be, it was in the sense of God's way. He wanted me found if it meant that he would have to do the search. It was as though he knew no one could convince me to him so he made the effort alone. At one point I was lost and confused along the path. I couldn't comprehend how I had not been found yet and therefore blamed everyone for giving up hope on me. I had assumed that God too had left me out in the cold but all along he was there. If he had not yelled for me I would not have known my own existence. Little did I know that while I grew weak with hunger he became willing to save me.

We were one together.....finally! I was home and peace filled my life from this point on. Nothing went without answers and I could see beyond the limit of my own sight. I knew that if I was alone in flesh that in spirit I was joined. When I would call for his assistance he would answer. Even if that answer didn't bring immediate results. That was O.K with me because I believed that he would eventually come through for me.

After I had accepted God as my personal Savior in June 22, 2009, I started to see blessings come my way. My husband and I had a well managed income and our stressors became minimal. I reenlisted in the Marine Corps and had received orders to move. My immediate family was still intact. Of course, we still had some unbearable problems but in the after math we jointly forgave and continued alongside one another.

I couldn't believe we were this fortunate. In less than one year we had experienced great job opportunities. Within this same time frame I had also been promoted to the rank of Sergeant in the Marine Corps and was holding one of the most critical process improvement billets. My job consisted of changing the way business was being done and assisting in making that change permanent based on the business goals. Not only was the position great but now I was being offered a college opportunity.

It wasn't long before the Marine Corps was paying for

my schooling at Lean Six Sigma College through NAVAIR located in Portsmouth, Virginia. For the second time in my life God had given me a career path. Upon graduation I was a well known Lean Six Sigma Practitioner. Here I was a 24 year old mother and wife with accomplishments in the medical field and a Lean Six Sigma Practitioner. I knew that I didn't do it alone---God was there.

I had stopped attending the same church as my husband so that he could focus on his musical talent and also because I was still a bit shy letting him see the soft side of me. I continued seeking God and made him my daily encouragement. Doing so gave me a thankful attitude. Now it was my turn to give back.

CHAPTER FIVE: SET IN STONE

"It is better to give than to receive", words that echoed in my thoughts. I wasn't willing to take anything for granted, especially in God's will. I considered myself as only a "Co-Owner" to every blessing, whether intangible or physical, that came my way. What that meant was that I would be content with what little was required and sow the rest to serve as a blessing for someone else.

It wasn't important for me to flash the latest fashion or have the best of the best in things. My heart was truly transformed. I wanted to put God where he put me, in other people's path. It was just a better feeling to watch a hopeless look turn into praise. It was like he wanted for me to continue down this journey without me having to carry the burden of the world. I began to be very thankful towards God for this.

Even through this phase I was aware of my need to continue educating myself with God. It wasn't long before I had come across one of the most important messages to mankind....the Ten Commandments. I was aware of the Ten Commandments before now but I had never paid much attention to the meaning. I saw the Ten Commandments as guidance if followed with faith but as evidence if followed by the desire of only the body. I was sure that they were evidence that would be served in court on Judgment Day.

As I continued to read down the list I could feel the importance. It wasn't like God was asking us to follow laws that we, ourselves, had not wanted for the soul. These laws were simple and to the point. As I read the story of Moses and the two tablets, which contained the Ten Commandments, a feeling of hope came over me. God had shown himself in person to Moses so that the world would know he was there. It was said that anyone who saw God would die but he had assured Moses that this would not be his fate. Beyond the laws I saw a bigger meaning----God appearing to this duty. That to me was "Hope".

If God could show himself to Moses then I could do the same in life. I needed to stand to my family. I needed to send the message myself. Delivering the hope that would show them that I was there for them. This was not going to be an easy mission because for years I had held a profound hate in separation towards our ways. I had become contempt with feeling like it wasn't possible. Now I had to take that extreme measure that once proved impossible. I was also somewhat filled with pride and held on to it long enough to make excuses for not acting on change sooner.

Before I could carry this journey and set the foundation in stone I needed God. I sought him for a way to overcome my pride because it had become my way of life. I didn't realize it until it came time for me to confront family matters. All I would tell myself was, "Well they don't care so why should I?" or "I'm not the major part of the issue". Now I was willing to put an end to it without question. So how did God answer me?

I went to church one Sunday morning and as I was thinking about how to approach my family without being too prideful the Pastor began talking about six things that God does not like. He continued to read a passage from Proverbs Chapter 6 verse 17 (King James Version) and it read (17) **"A proud look, a lying tongue, and hands that shed innocent blood"**. The Pastor continued explaining the list, once he was finished reading verses 17-19 he concluded with "...Pride is the first step to a fall..." That was the icing on the cake. That was it! I was influencing failure by holding on to my pride that I had assumed was excusable.

By the end of the sermon I was motivated with hope. I didn't want to keep casting stones in situations where I felt, in my opinion, was fit for one. Instead God had sent me the message to "Set in stone" a solution. A concrete ground for our ways to have crossing paths. We didn't have to keep going towards opposed routes. It wasn't fate that was keeping us separated but our "proud look". God had given me an answer with the answer.

It was specific and to the point, he did not seem upset with me for praying in receiving an answer in that same manner---specific. I began to contact my family in hopes of having a family reunion. I did not want to tell them the purpose of having one because I didn't want to wake any buried hate. So I knew I had to be tactful and careful in my introduction. I wanted to save the best for the dinner table. Where I was hoping we could sit together and be thankful to God. I had also prepared a small, to the point, speech for the family without any bias opinion from either one of us.

I wanted to introduce God and show to them that we could be a living testimony. If he could change me at my worst then he could do the same for us as well. I began to communicate with them one person at a time and set this occasion in "stone". I was glad that some had agreed but still others were not accepting of the idea. I wasn't disappointed though because it was better to reach some than none at all.

Within weeks some of us had reached closure with one another. Of course, most of that came with apologies and forgiveness. It wasn't long before words became positive and we maintained endless communication. We still had a long way to go but what was important was that we were getting there together. Some we're still pessimistic but they weren't left behind just placed ahead in our prayers. This was an awesome feeling.

There was still one important person to reach---Mom. She had been bearing the ultimate pain. She had watched her children drift away from each other. She had attempted to bring us together but she had put most of her strength on taking most of the blame. I remember her once saying "I want you all to get along even if I'm left behind". She had raised us as a single mother and needed to see that it meant a lot to us. As siblings we were coming together but what are we without her? I'm sure we all pointed a finger her way but over time we could see that we had been pointing in the wrong direction.

As mentioned in the fifth commandment: "Honor thy Father and thy Mother..." It was our obligation to have our Mother involved in our lives. Our entire closure depended on her. How to reach her though? I could see the skepticism forming in our looks as we attempted to approach this matter as a family. It was like we had preferred for someone to stand up and just say "I'll talk to her". We had never spoken on a sentimental level with our Mother before and at this point in her life she was drowning in hopelessness.

I had at one point reached out to her to assure her that we could come together as a family. Her immediate reaction was pessimistic and it was at that point that I was overwhelmed with negative factors. It was a fair argument on her end but it was taking a toll on me. I had still maintained communication but it seemed like I was getting nowhere. It was a vicious cycle of "If's" and "Buts'". So eventually I too had given up trying.

It wasn't a wise decision on my behalf. Our communication had completely ceased and I had allowed it to end abruptly. No matter what, I had failed to make ends meet. I should have been more understanding of the pressure she was under and the circumstances that had kept her a prisoner. It was as though I was trying to convince the jury of her innocence but yet her testimony was in support of punishment. It wasn't long before her sentence was declared and she was taken away. It was as though she had briefly looked back at me with a blank stare. It was a stare that sought a smile but accepted sorrow.

While avoiding her I was also growing angry again with my husband. He seemed to be making his own decisions and I mine without understanding. Patience was rare but tension grew stronger. The fights became unbearable and eventually we had quit on trying. When we were apart I always felt a bit more at ease so it only seemed reasonable to give "quitting" a fair chance into action.

I felt terrible about all of this but I admit I needed the strength to conquer this barrier. I'm sure that over time they had also learned to build walls and hold in emotions. It was the only thing we had in common this entire time. We were persistent to change and buried feelings too deep from one another. Nothing was too far for God, this I was sure of. I eventually brought out my concerns in prayer to avoid drifting from accepting change. Likewise, I firmly believed that it wasn't over for us until God sets it in stone.

CHAPTER SIX: THIS TOO SHALL PASS

The storm was still amid our problems. It had made sight very foggy and I wasn't even sure if we would ever see the calm. At this point I was just more accepting of the circumstances. It just appeared to be an impossible task to go from a distant family to a loving one. Oh well! Right?...not at all. It was far from over.

Right when it felt like the storm was blowing over another thunder warned me of a close impact nearby. It was like I was waiting on the sound of the thunder and counting the seconds to the next strike so that I may determine how close to the storm I was sitting....Yes that's right---Sitting. I had refused to put any more effort into being the Alpha Dog in the pack.

God wasn't having any of it though. My marriage had met with the end of its path and my divorce was now finalized. My career was rocky because of the impact of my now terminated marriage. We were at wits end with each other. I wasn't about to let this be another issue for me to take the lead on either. My shoulders were wearing down with heavy burdens. I was far from weighting my odds because it wasn't long before our buried hatred started to tear my immediate family apart.

Long story short, Social Services were questioning me in what was perceived to have been just to create turmoil by an "unknown caller". As a mother it was an insult to have your hard work and independence questioned. My children were now taken away for the weekend until the court could meet. I had been in trial in my home, with my siblings, my mother, my career, and now with my children.

No! I wasn't giving up but there was a bit of hopelessness in my thoughts.

I had never cried as much as I did trying to work with the investigators and the court system for my image. The hardest thing for me had always been to show weakness or cry in front of anyone. I had built barriers along my lifespan to include not being easily read. So through this phase I had cut communication with my family and my command. I was feeling overwhelmed with doubts. To make matters worse, my now ex-husband had apologized for his role in the hurt but that wasn't going to get me my children back.

I needed to find patience and let God handle it but it was easier said than done. I was beginning to believe that I was the "eye of the storm". No matter how hard I try to climb and stay above ground level there was always something or someone else pulling me down. I just wanted to have things my way just one time----JUST ONE TIME.

Was I asking for too much God? Where have I failed? Why me? Loads of questions filled my prayers. I wasn't accepting destiny as an excuse for the unending path of problems. I was becoming weak in my own strength. The storm had been so unpredictable..... So God what now?

By the beginning of the following week all my tears and all my questions were receiving answers. The investigators found no fault with me and instead filed a citation against the accuser. I had received physical custody of my children and I was given time from work to take care of home. To say the least, God was guiding me in the storm. He had placed the right individuals so that they may find the strength to deal with my weakness. I couldn't have been more contempt with it all.

I remember how I stood in court not really hearing the case nor the investigators because my mind was more on having to hear more bad news. My legs where shaking and head lowered into my hands. It wasn't until the words "....physical custody of the children will be returned to the mother..." that a loud sigh came over me and my nerves started to reach calm. I remember walking out of the court room looking over at my command in gratefulness because they had stood with me during the storm keeping me conscious of the positives.

After returning home with my children I received a call from my mom. I wasn't really prepared to get back to an emotional level with her but I was glad to know that even through it all the motherly love was there. We talked solely about the kids coming back home. We were careful not to pick old scabs and instead buried those conversations in the past. Regardless, here we were again--talking.

I have to be honest, of all people my mom would have been at the bottom of my list for support impact. Our history was written and we weren't always willing to see eye to eye and thus kept clear of one another. I was in awe to know that she was in the storm looking for me with concern and that when she wasn't sure where to find me she at least knew to pray for me. I wasn't lost because she prayed, she prayed because in her I was not lost. If there is no greater evidence of God's way then tell me---WHAT IS?

My ex-husband on the other hand could not find comfort in his own actions and asked for forgiveness. I forgave him for one reason and one reason only; because everything goes only in God's will. We kept neutral and distant for our child which gave me some peace of mind. I've always told him that "We are not bad people; we are just bad for each other". Thus, the important factor was our child and ensuring the highest quality of welfare.

What kind of person would I be not to forgive? Although he had his actions I cannot portray myself into perfection. This was a moment where I had endured much needless pain but it was beyond my own personal persecution. At this point I had to live by God's wisdom and forgive as I would want for myself during my own faults.

Regardless, no human being has the strength to change God's will. It's like disobeying your parent's wish and right after you have made your own rules you begin to find yourself deeper in trouble and all your parent can say is "I told you so!". Soon we are left with guilt and accepting that we had only failed ourselves. Besides, no finger pointing could make up for the inflicted pain so in God's hands I left the will to carry through.

By the end of the second court date my ex-husband and I had leaned away from hate and discontent. We weren't trustful being in one another's company (I definitely didn't trust him) but we had ensure that we exercised our strength in being mature parent's to safeguard my youngest child's "Parent-Child relationship". I tell you, I wanted nothing more than to avoid my ex-husband all together but this is where my test would be graded.

I spent many times saying that I could let God take charge of my life and guard me through any obstacle and I needed to do just that. Even while my world seemingly fell apart I prayed and laid my burdens for God. It was really difficult at first because I felt like retaliating towards my ex-husband but seeing how he started to feel the pressure of guilt I knew that God had the matter in his hands. I also knew that my judgment would only fuel disaster but God's will...his will always triumph.

Sometimes we go through a storm and find ourselves getting comfortable with the idea of it destroying everything in its path to include our hopes. We let the physical environment have a much greater impact in our spiritual world until we become lost when the physical one is foggy. I learned the importance of putting God ahead in my life not just in the calm but in the STORM. The problems came and went because with God nothing is impossible. The greatest part of faith is realizing that......THIS TOO SHALL PASS!

CHAPTER SEVEN: FAMILY REUNION

By the end of the month following my last court for my children my mom had traveled down to pick up the kids. I remember waiting at the airport for her flight to arrive and only hoping that the effort we had already put in our communication would only show its strength. My oldest brother and I had waited two hours for the flight to only find that she was on a later flight. So we waited some more this time anticipation grew.

She finally appeared through the exit way and came over with a low tone "Hello". We started heading towards baggage claims. I could tell from my peripheral vision that she was observing my every move. The way I walk, talk, and communicate. It was as though she was trying to find evidence of our mother-to-daughter relationship. I attempted to break the ice of silence by joking about her bag being lost.

I'm sure to her it was a surprise to see the woman I have grown to become. She was finally letting loose and allowing the little communication that was being provided. I could tell along the way that she noticed that I was more talkative with my oldest brother around. I was not doing so purposely but somewhere in our past finger pointing we had become strangers to one another. This was the beginning for us to rebuild with the very stones we once threw in hate.

We had finally arrived at my house and she was starring at everything with wonder. She had never seen me in my uniform and my work environment before. Although by this time I had already served a full contract to the military and near the end of my second (six years of honorable service). We talked about the rank structure, military words, the uniform, deployments and so on. It was pleasing for me to share with her this side of me that I've loved and conquered. A place where I had been for the past six years.

As I had expected to happen, she started to veer our conversations into the Mother-Daughter aspects of life. She politely asked me about how I was doing outside of my military life and of course I said "Fine". She briefly continued with telling me how she recalls moments when I would come home from school go straight to my room and study. She explained how she never worried about me because she could see beyond words that my priorities were straight. Even more, I started to feel happy to know that she could have that much confidence in me.

Well of course my home was spotless and she was appreciative of that but what wouldn't leave my mind was how it wasn't the things surrounding us that she was interested in, it was ME. Though I had spent some time cleaning and ensuring it would meet her specifications I failed to see that I was the reason she came to visit. What I do and the choices I make in life are what she is most concern with. Wow! How could I have missed out on the important part of her motherly ways...

Sometimes we worry too much about what our parents may think and how they may pursue changes in us. We would wipe every stain and sweep every room when our parents are ready to visit but as soon as they step foot outside and no longer in sight we return to our normal routine of things. We accommodate our situations based on what helps us feel better. Then I began to think of the ways of my own faith. Was I treating my faith in the same manner?

Really sit back and think this through for a second. Are we living in God when we assume that we have understood the meaning of faith? I needed to take some time for myself and see where I stood in my life and in my faith. I looked long and hard and began to read on the ways of God because I did not want to falter in his love for me. Sometimes we can make ourselves believe that everything we do is right by God because we become the jury in our own trials.

It really concerned me to feel this way. All along I was sure that I was doing right by God....well in some areas I had but there were some situations where I would just feel I was correct in my actions simply because I was "Provoked". At times like that I wouldn't bring the issues and faults to God because, in my own understanding, I was convinced that he sees them in the same manner. Fact is I should've known better not to lean in my own understanding.

That wasn't all, what came to light the most was knowing that when I thought God was coming by to visit, of course a figure of speech, I would clean my act, thoughts, and perception of things. Every spot and blemish was concealed but what happens when we set God aside for a second? We begin to lose our ways and more obstacles seem to make their way in. It is then that we wonder why our path is rocky.

I could hear an alarm sound in my very being and an inner voice that reminded me of my own selfishness. I didn't want to be of God part-time. Faith isn't a nine in the morning to five at night job that we can rest from on the weekends. I was sure that God needed to be a leading role in my life.

Just like my mom, God wasn't coming for a visit just to see my environment but to see about ME. Though fine silverware and clean cloths look great it isn't enough to buy any of God's love because he desires our faith. There is such a thin line in having faith because we can easily misguide ourselves with excuses. Well I can assure you that it does nothing good for God.

This was my opportunity to transform into what God needed from me by not concealing my true actions. Just like he isn't blind to our suffering, he also knows when we are cleaning our home but not our ways. Well I didn't want to be naive by just preparing my home with the finest things. From this point on I was sure to prepare myself so that I too may sit on the right hand of his throne.

CHAPTER EIGHT: OPPORTUNITY KNOCKS

Finally, I had built the strength to start over after a long divorce and the stressful court proceedings. Although with opportunity came preparing to enhance my military career my chances seemed slim. Somehow though, it seemed my command was not prepared in sending me on any deployments. That only left me going from work to home and vice-versa.

At this point I began to wear down with loneliness. My oldest two children had returned back with my mom for the school year and my youngest was going back and forth between me and her father. I would come home to a dark and empty house. It no longer felt like home. I no longer had anyone waiting for me in this house. I found more excitement going to work to be around peers.

Eventually going to work only wore me out. I couldn't sleep very well at night anymore. The times that I did manage to sleep more than two hours I only awoke to the sounds of an empty place. There were so many opportunities out there that I sought but now it seemed that success no longer had a good taste.

I wanted to share everything with a family waiting for me to come home. I wasn't necessarily depressed in this environment but I really hated feeling like this house was no longer a home. It was finely decorated and fitted for a family of five but yet I was the only one there. Soon my couch took the purpose of my bed and the living room was the only room I occupied.

I was trying to regain strength after a long divorce and the extensive issues therein. I knew "Going on" was the route to take but now as a single mother I had to lean on family for help. It was not a bad thing but they lived far away. This meant that my kids too would be miles from reach. I began to miss when the sound of my children would fill the room.

How did I get between these dark walls built in a secluded area? I was looking for opportunity and had wonderful successes in life but now my once proclaimed immediate family was torn. My command was reluctant in allowing me purpose to serve again due to concerns of family stressors. Now I was wearing guilt for my family and a uniform that had lost its battle patterns. All of this because in this very home we had given up on greater opportunity.

Now looking back I noticed how we were one body. If the head rejected the body then it could no longer stand strong. So many days had been spent on procrastination. Everything was scheduled for "tomorrow", never did we handle problems at the appropriate times. Eventually "tomorrow" no longer came and opportunity ceased to knock. It was then that I got my fair taste of "time waits for no one".

I became anxious to bring light back into my home and knock down those walls. I had taken yesterday for granted when arguments and disagreement shattered the foundation. Now my family was torn in pieces. Our focus was on "tomorrow" bringing on a change. The sort of solution that only prolonged our problems. In the end we had not taken in consideration those obvious chances.

I attended church, this time to minimize the impact of my now confusing situation. I was looking for that answer to bring satisfaction to a once blossomed flower pulled by its roots. I wanted my FAMILY back so I prayed for wisdom to conquer the things uncertain in this moment.

I wanted another chance to regain the health of my family....I had my ear to the door as not miss that opportunity knocking again. Of course, we all await that wonderful sound. We search high and low for opportunity to our desired hopes. It took me some time to realize that "opportunity" exist primarily with effort.

How I took all this for granted. It was a stressful heartache. There were so many lessons learned in this for me. I tell you; from that point on I refused to use ignorance as a backbone. I was now on a mission...I was going to recover my family back. If it meant knocking and hoping they'll answer to my voice when I do.

I was going to pay a visit even if they least expected one. Once the knock was served with an answer I was sure to have my arms extended for a hug. I would then enter and as a family we will sit at a dinner table again and pray together. It was all just a matter of time.

I had enough with taking home for granted with placing ignorance where there stood a chance of recovery. My ignorance made the appearance of no visitors. NO MORE! I had prepared a place where we could enter and not be ashamed of our ways. I had shed light on my faults so that nothing was left to be swept under the rug.

This time around my approaches to things were different. I was now paying close attention for that knock of opportunity. It was about keeping this family together and protecting our home from further separation. It was time to lay the foundation properly in this house.

It's much like God's promising word in which he tells us that he will stand at the door hoping to see if we stood nearby listening for him to knock (Revelations 3:20).

" Behold, I stand at the door and knock. If anyone hears My voice and opens the door, I will come in to him and dine with him, and he with Me"

Well now I was learning to become prepared to listen for this great opportunity. Preparing for that moment when we could sit down as a family. He will be able to see the sign on my door that warns evil that God is the head of my household.

I am sure he will find my house and see my front porch light on because all along I had been waiting. He will then be glad that of many houses on the block he had finally found one that had stood through the storm....and as a FAMILY we will enter God's kingdom. Hand in hand, husband and wife, parent and child, together sharing victory in this place we would finally call home.

CHAPTER NINE: HE'S WORKING IT OUT

My youngest daughter was now turning three years old. Her father and I were planning out a good birthday for her. He had finally decided on getting her an outdoors playground. Of course, we had to work together to put the playground together. Finally, when it was assembled we called her outside. She had run as fast as her little footsteps could go and headed outdoors filled with excitement.

It was a great sight to see. She was glowing with joy knowing the playground was hers. Here she was unsure of which part to conquer. It was amusing to watch her jump from one side to the other in a matter of seconds.

When the night drew near I said "good-bye" to my daughter, she wasn't adapting to the idea though. Since my divorce from her father she started to become sad seeing either of us leave. She would cry with confusion in her voice. It was her way of saying, "Why can't you stay?" I would stare at her and pass the situation as a moment but it bothered me a lot.

She was too young to understand why Mommy and Daddy no longer resided together. I never attempted to explain it to her nor call my house her home or vice-versa. I tried as much as I could to either avoid further confusion or explaining the situation.

Her father then began to tell me when she would call for "mommy" on random occasions during his care, this included in her sleep. I became worry she would have separations anxiety. To her we were the confused ones. Here we had a three year old instructing us to "take off your shoes" and proceeding to explain that we needed a blanket to go "night-night". All this information because she could not understand why one parent needed to leave just to rest for the night.

Eventually she was forcing us to spend more time taking her to places together. We had to ensure her mental growth as much as her physical being. I would hear her sing songs and then move her concentration on her siblings. Oh how she missed them too.

My oldest son was the leader of the pack. He was always teaching his sisters new things. He was focused on sports and becoming "Mommy's little Marine". There were times I would catch him wearing some of my uniform items which I found pretty interesting to watch. My middle child became the "Girlie Girl". She was a 'fashion-ista'. She had taken her youngest sister by the wings and helped her embrace "dress up time".

They got along very well. They filled a room with all sorts of amusements. Just a unique laughing experience for all of us. Now I was telling one child she would have to wait to spend time with the other two and to the others that soon we could be back in one home again.

I was devastated beyond words. My babies! Separated by the choices of the adults responsible for the stability of their home. I was holding back tears of disappointment. God what has happened?...just help me pull through. My kids were being affected and I couldn't stop it.

This is one of the worst experiences for any mother. I would carry a look of worry and sadness when they would ask about one another. I could not even look my own children in the eyes to tell them the facts. When they would ask questions about each other or us as parents I would answer while walking away or simply changing the subject.

I had been prepared to take on many challenges in life but definitely not this. This was overbearing, I knew I was going to keep God very busy. Every second I was asking him for strength and every day I was asking for answers. I was sure by now I had his schedule full with my burdens.

I was trying to cope with it but instead I had settled with not talking about the situation at hand. I was actually forcing myself to believe that it wasn't happening. I would turn away as though they did not notice the separation. I was approaching my children as though they couldn't see beyond the words of "It's OK".

All these years I thought being a mother was only about teaching your kids right from wrong. Taking the time to be the first influence in their lives. Rewarding them according to their actions. Sadly I had forgotten one thing...they were teaching me. Even through the small fights they would have with one another they still knew to forgive and forget.

It felt like God was working through my children. He had taken these innocent individuals to keep me focused on what is more important. Those "opinions" or that "point-of-view" I threw in arguments, they were worthless. Common ground only came when those factors were set aside and we gave understanding----only understanding.

My children were teaching me at the most critical time in our lives. All those constant "Why Mommy?" woke reality for me...they were right, so right. We had put so many reasons of excuses into our arguments and many more emphases on our own understanding but looking back at those times the fact was "WHY!!!"

CHAPTER TEN: SECOND CHANCE

I just wanted a second chance to see everything fall back into place. I hated that so much was happening like this. It was difficult attempting to calm the rough waters. God was the only thing holding me right in my path. But soon, I was struggling again.

Growing up I had been exposed to drugs, alcohol, and other habits by my peers. But I was never influenced by "peer pressure". I found it amusing to watch others making attempts to convince me into "just one drink" or "try it one time only". I was proud of myself at being able to say "no". All those times I could've leaned towards one gateway or another but didn't.

I was sober in my mental state of mind and nothing could change that. My morals were firm and my actions showed just that. Eventually I found myself looking back at those years as though I had been missing out on something. As though I had a chance to sober up with those very things my peers had found logic in.

Here I was divorced, my kids separated, in a lonely home, working with little or no energy. So where could I lean on. Yes, God was my dose of hope but I didn't want hope---I wanted peace. I wanted to run far away from all these issues. Those problems that reminded me that I would be alone in this world again.

Less than four months later I was drinking and smoking cigarettes. It felt great to be angry one moment and liberated the next. Even if that freedom was short lived but it was better than not having it at all. I knew God wanted me to keep my narrow path but I didn't want it anymore because I was far too depressed to remain constant. That wasn't the last of things though.

I saw a different person in myself, she was now a stranger. But all along I didn't think she was this close to disaster but she was looking back at me. My choices to do these things were because, in my thoughts, I just wanted God to move on to someone else. If he was going to waste anymore of his own time it was definitely on me. There had to be someone else out there more deserving for a second chance.

I went down to the lakefront a lot since then. There I could sit on a swing and stare off into the lake. I could watch the water flow with such calm but I knew that beneath it had a story. The wind would caress my face all while the sound would whisper in my ear. I could feel the touch of nature.

On the flip side, I couldn't feel anyone reaching out for me. No one touching my very soul to remind me that I was far from hopelessness. I went from one drink to two, then from two to a sleeping aid. It was tough. The cigarettes were more like a challenge. I would attempt to consume a little more each day. No one ever noticed...no one!

I was still that joy to be around, that friend with wisdom to pass, that strong woman. Oh, but how that portrait was far from being true. Depression was kicking me right in the face. It had me one drink at a time and one cigarette after another. It was not very long after that I looked down towards my feet and realized how far I've walked alone lost.

One day, while I sat on this swing by the lakefront a young adult male approached me. He had seen the cigarette in my hand and asked if he could use my lighter. I've never had anyone ask me anything in the nature of cigarettes. I briefly looked up at him and pulled the lighter from my purse. He lit his cigarette, returned the lighter and left. Less than ten minutes later he had returned to borrow the lighter again.

I looked at the freshly new cigarette in his hand. I was prepared for his question, so I reached down into my purse again and I pulled the lighter out. Once again, he lit his cigarette, returned the lighter and began on his way. Before he was fully out of sight I called him back with a "Excuse me". He looked back and waited for the rest. It was then that I said "Here, you can have my lighter and my cigarettes". He looked confused and asked "Why?" and I replied with "I don't smoke".

He wondered what I was meaning because he had watched me smoking. He eventually said, with a sound of laughter in his voice, "...but you were just smoking". With that I said, "Yes I was but I decided it would be my last cigarette". The conversation continued with him asking "Are you sure you can quit that quickly?!"....my answer "I don't have to worry about quitting anymore". Proudly I stood up from the swing put the cigarette in my hand out and walked away.

For nearly a month I had consumed my life in poorly executed choices. All because I didn't think I no longer deserved a second chance. Right when my faith was growing strong my world came collapsing again. I didn't blame God, I blamed myself. I was angry at ME! For allowing room for the wrong people to enter my life. For thinking that life had a backdoor.

During the most depressing time in my life I had felt as

if this large town were only four walls. I couldn't hide from what was happening. I didn't know how to ask for help. I was asking God to leave me here for the moment. Regardless, God still answered. This complete stranger had reminded me that I was not myself. Not only that, but I was not going to proclaim these choices as an addiction.

I finally phoned a good friend and let all my pain out. I was beginning to feel strong again. As I was explaining my pain I was realizing how small they really were. Those problems were just temporary but I was acting on permanent decisions. After talking with my close friend I also came to see that my story did not need to end like such. My kids needed a role-model, doing things out of depression wasn't good judgment.

I finally got in my car, turn my music on and before driving away I stared myself in the rearview mirror. With watery eyes I smiled a bit at my effort to leave that "stranger" behind. A part of me that was only a character in disguise. As I started to head home, I slowed my car down to look at the lake one last time for the day and to myself I said "I am not a quitter".

CHAPTER ELEVEN: CLEARING AWAY FROM DEBRIS

I was still putting effort in rebuilding the stability of my home, my faith, and my own sanity. I had been wiping away tears of sorrow for far too long. It was now time to see beyond the foggy moments that placed such limitations. I was preparing to clear away from all of the debris.

I had spent so much time focusing on what was affecting me and not noticing my own involvement. I am sure that my actions weren't solely the only failure in the equation but a small portion makes a large contribution. It's more like the popular saying of "Two wrongs don't make it right". I guess this is what we call "maturity" in the experience.

My finger pointing has ceased abruptly during this phase. I was still disappointed with my own actions. I had been a part of the hate in my family, in my marriage, and within myself. I was entertaining problems that really had no goal. I was keeping God busy with hopes of steering my path only because I thought I had 80% of his support.

Wow, how we convince ourselves that God pick sides as we seek the popular vote for an excuse to our actions. What about that 20% of risk that we accept? Does it become undermined? Well I realized that the risk percentage included my kids, our home, and our family. It was the small things that counted the most, still does.

I was now keeping my positive attitude and actions on the outward to keep my own sanity. I never cut communication with my ex-husband though it was not always what I desired. We still had small arguments here and there. Most of which went back into the past and actions thereafter. It was like we had to remind one another of where we currently stood---that is DIVORCED.

The pain caused during our marriage has lived past our own partnership. It was gradually becoming the only focus of conversations. I hated talking with him because it was eventually stressing me out. It had become so overbearing that I began to attend counseling for myself. I spend all my counseling times just talking about how I felt he wasn't going to go on until he saw that my life took a turn for the worst.

I felt that way because nothing beyond our words spoke of understanding or forgiveness. I also took my counseling sessions to explain how I no longer knew what more I wanted from my life. My counselor would ask me questions about my career but I no longer called it a "career" just a temporary stepping stone.

He would eventually reassure me that my family wasn't torn apart just recouping from tension. Regardless, I was cleaning up all the past and moving forward. I was taking a new route in my judgment calls. I was willing to pick up all these pieces one at a time.

Counseling helped a bit of course but I didn't always tell him what was on my mind. The reason I didn't always talked all my problems in this small room was because I wanted to keep God for those "impossible" moments. The things I didn't say during my counseling I mentioned in my prayers and carried with my actions.

Even with talking all my concerns through I still felt like a big gap existed in my heart. That's a place my counselor couldn't reach because it was far too sore for his words of reassurance. It was time to admit that even though I hated my ex-husband, I also loved him. My nights seemed empty with silence and my days with little energy to focus.

I tried to keep busy by drawing some pictures for good friends or even playing some games on my computer but it wasn't enough. I couldn't understand what was happening nor why. I had let go of a part of me that only provided stressors in my life. I had set myself free to find a place where I can truly be complete. I didn't understand why all of a sudden I didn't feel like moving on.

I had packed all those portraits that were marked by the past, the house was rebuilt for a single parent....what now? I mean, this was all an outcome of a hateful relationship. I still disliked a lot about him and vice versa. The hate was apparent.

I continued to attend my counseling sessions as scheduled and finally I asked the question "Do you think I still need counseling?". My counselor answered with "Well do you?". At first I had taken his answer as a dodge to mine but it was then I noticed that my life depended on my own decision. Why was I asking him about my path ahead!

He does not have the answers to life just has the words that serve encouragement. It wasn't his choice or something he had a control of. The answer was obvious but I was ignoring it because of my own frustration with trying to comprehend the situations. I ended this counseling session as my final one. I did not schedule another because I didn't need counseling that helped relive the past that only awoke hatred. Instead, I was going to keep leaning on God to help me find that unique love that conquers peace.

On the flip side, the sessions assisted me a lot when I

needed to release my anger. It was well suited for those stressful times but I was now beyond those moments. I was now trying to figure out where I needed to sweep to clear the debris from the past. I was recovering a new strength so that finally...just finally I could show more appreciation to what God was already providing.

I had once given up on opportunities to enhance positive outcomes for that negative attitude. I was not always wrong but I had definitely encouraged a revolving cycle of hate. No more though, that was it for me. Hatred seems to have a strong ability to consume time and effort. It had brought me into a place where I had to leave behind someone I loved because I had grown to hate him.

I accepted that we had both lost this fight. Not one stood above the other of "Moving Forward". I could tell we stood still awaiting signs that implied another chance though we didn't find comfort finding one. I was truly heartbroken but it was time to give hatred a break and keep clear of the debris that clustered our choices.

CHAPTER TWELVE: ENGAGING IN TRUTH

(Deep Breath) One chapter following another. I am not going to make assumptions of being the only one going through some hardship although it felt like I was alone in the feeling. I know I should've opened up much sooner. Expressed my thoughts without the fights or finger pointing. It would've have been better to take my thoughts and engage them in the truth with peace.

I had always been strong willed and difficult to influence. Well it got me nowhere so it was time to lean on listening more. It is said that the "truth shall set you free". Time to find how free it would prove. I was not against the facts just anxious to see resolution maintain its stance.

It was not long before my ex-husband had asked to talk things through. To acknowledge lack of partnership as it should have been preserved. He wanted to meet to "try" and see what develops. I was skeptical but I was also willing to give a chance at a simple conversation.

We had not proven to each other the basis of good conversation just yet. It didn't matter though; we were only "trying", making an attempt to see on the same level of understanding. It shouldn't hurt to be confident in accomplishing such a conversation.

He wanted to go to a restaurant. I could already tell that his intent wasn't just to talk. I only say this because during the phone conversation he had a sense of urgency. Sort of like "Please meet me there" or "don't say NO" kind of urgency. Not one that sounded an alarm though.

So there we were sitting at the restaurant and ordering food. Our daughter was tagging along as well. He looked at me and I looked over at him. I was laughing with him but deep down I kind of felt like I might be regretting this. I had spent so much time planning the "moving forward" phase that being this close to him was like putting life into the past.

He, in my thoughts, was the PAST. One I loved dearly but hated repeatedly. It was such an awkward place to be. Of course, in the moment I was focusing on accomplishing peace. So even if that was how I felt I had placed it into the back burner. We didn't need to fight again over our individually buried pain.

Well the looks continued and the conversations were closed-ended. We couldn't keep a good topic afloat. Regardless, we were communicating and not fighting. I was applauding the effort to say the least. I caught myself starring at random things to pass the silence that came from the simple answers.

He eventually got up and headed towards the waiter area with our daughter following behind him. She was just anxious to move about so I took the opportunity to make a quick walk to the restroom. I headed back out with a deep sigh and sat back down with our daughter. I looked over to him and saw a look of nervousness. At that point I realized with a thought of *"Oh my GOD, NO he isn't!"*

In no time the noise in the restaurant had filled with silence and on lookers eyeballing in my direction. He walked with obvious questions on his mind. It was as though he was wondering whether his soon to be actions should be executed. My heart just skipped a beat.

He stood centering himself between myself and the staff and began to talk. This time it was words of appreciation. Wow, REALLY! Five years and this was the first time he expressed serious feelings. I was looking at him and then down to the table and back to him. I couldn't maintain focus.

It was immediately after he gave a quick narrative story about our time together that he pops the question. The words "Will you marry me?" shocked me. I immediately stood to my feet, nodded my head, looked down at my hand as he held on to it and watched the mark of a lifetime. I had, without hesitation said "yes".

All this time had passed and he was one I was willing to hate with a passion. I never thought I could lean back into my feelings because I thought I had convinced myself at ignoring them. He was the one I blamed for such an experience in the past.

On the flip side, marriage should not be sacrificed for misunderstanding. It is suppose to serve as the foundation to a long term partnership. But somehow we had managed to neglect the vows of marriage. We were ultimately the reason for our own failure in this matter. All that time and yet we waited for change with procrastination.

Eventually having so much time on your hands from waiting seems like a waste. You separate from each other and lose that common ground. Sooner or later the finger pointer starts to lead to discontent. In no time, your best friend is turned worst enemy.

Right when two people think that they built the strength to move forward the problems become consistent. It is then that we forget what brought us together as husband and wife…God. Our devotion to God and the upholding of our home.

We had gone through all those problems because we had failed to see the body God made whole. These very factors were the break of our home. When we compromised our commitment we left room for hate to destroy the foundation.

I was now engaged to the same man that I once thought was a reflection of my past. The truth was simple, I was still waiting. Though sometimes hatefully, I stood nearby for us to look back and see for ourselves what was really there…our destiny!

CHAPTER THIRTEEN: IN GOD WE TRUST

God was working in some very mysterious ways. He had showed us how our own personal decisions had affected the true intent he had for us. For five years me and my now fiancé had created turmoil. Living by the means of our flesh while despising obvious proof to do otherwise.

Enough years to have served as appropriate timing to recover but we never had. It took us hurting one another, stretching the hate into other matters in our lives, and finally letting go to see what stood before us. Right when we had thought God was driving fate we had influenced separation. It was not long before we were disturbed by the outcomes.

Looking back, it was like we had leaned on the world to convince us we were right. The fact was; they only heard a one sided story or extreme explanations due to the building hate. We had compiled scenes of that "Not good for each other" among those who knew us. We were like that immature couple not ready to embrace logic.

I will not say that I thought that the outside opinions were wrong but I do know that they were not fully supported. They definitely had a lot of reason to make such conclusion because we had pushed the facts for them. They were split between the both of us. Somehow, we listened to those opinions and made enemies of one another.

Like I have mentioned earlier, it was not those on the outside looking in that were the problem. It was us on the inside opening the door for their views to impact our judgments of the marriage. We had made room in our relationship to be split in our hopes and understandings. It took some time but eventually we started to feel the burden of leaving half of ourselves with the other.

At this point, outside opinion was just a memoir. A book of stories that some people held as fresh news in their gossip. But no longer serves as advice to our now reestablished environment. They had their own lives to proclaim but we had finally taken the time to take a hold of our own. The bible tells us:

" What therefore God hath joined together, let not man put asunder "

It wasn't until we started trusting in God that we saw a new meaning. It was only after we appreciated life the same way we had once embraced war that we saw our true love. All along it had existed and was only awaiting a spark.

It was crazy to come to this realization because even now I could go back to those five years with some resentment toward our decisions. Five years where we were lost....but today, we have one another. We learned to forgive and forget just like that.

God was definitely that turning point for us. The moment I put God in my life and he was obeying God's true words we had found trust together. I am not sure how this story has impacted you. Maybe we are that "crazy" couple by now but if you ask me...I'll say we were just "Normal". That's right, because in the end we had walked in the same path most have crossed.

The path paved by our concrete decisions that are supported by selfishness. We were lost as we attempted to conquer common sense. The best part of all of this is that no matter what, God waited patiently. He allowed sometime for us to acknowledge that our own ways wouldn't accomplish positive resolution.

God was looking on as we placed our ignorance but right when we turned away from each other he stepped in. He was teaching us a lesson but not separating us. For this I thank him because I do believe deep down that if I had gone on without closure I would have never been happy. I am especially glad we no longer have to go through the negative motions.

Though this may sound harsh, I was glad God had pinned us against our will. He had briefly looked down at us with his hands crossed and watched as we struggled being without the other. He didn't step in sooner because he knew that we "had all the answers to life". Fairly, he let us see for ourselves our lack of appreciation.

God was just waiting for the right moment for us to place our trust in him. We still had some doubt of our love possibility but God knew just when to mend those pieces. Eventually God reached down and pushed just a bit, then again some more. It continued until I was back in the arms that once filled my heart with emptiness as my hateful words pushed further impact.

If God had not served a fine taste of judgment we would have maintained our focus on outside opinion. We would have continued trusting in our own views and of those who only conclude with half a story. Oh, but there is a greater being who brought some calm. It was the trust in God that built peace in our hearts. They say **"God is love"** so what better love than one you can trust.

CHAPTER FOURTEEN: SICK AND TIRED

So much progression was being accomplished with moving ahead in faith. I never would have imagined the extent of wisdom derived from believing so gratefully. When a person can grow strong mentally with wisdom they become physically stable even in sickness. It's a stability that pushes through those aches and pain or that tiredness.

We conquer faith as a transformation, which is fine, but look at how it drives your walk, talk, and even your heart. I may be taking this aspect to a different level of understanding but look at how faith changes us. It is nearly amazing. Just look at how easy it is to spot a person with faith. Ever stood among a group of people and with some observation you can just point that one individual who is building in God's grace?

I once stood before a group of people and watched an elderly woman just stand from her seat to help a small child to a chair. Not only was she in the worst health imaginable but her physical body moved with pain. Every step was one she had to think about trying again but no matter what she pushed passed it.

It's amazing how God works, really it is. It made me wonder about an older sister who I worried would be counting her days. Since my joining the Marine Corps she had been in and out of the hospital. She suffered from numerous health problems. I've attempted at appearing to be calm when talking with her but deep down I worried I would have to watch her leave right before my eyes.

There were times when I noticed she had no hope of

getting better or even making it past another birthday. A few years ago we had sat in her home and talked about life after death. We had wondered how heaven would be and whether it had existed. Of course, this was during a time when I had questioned God's existence.

Well, I had joked about left-hand people and the "you know what they say". She eventually replied with, "Since I know I am going to die first, if I end up in heaven I'll make sure you dream of a rabbit but if in hell it'll be of a turtle". Oh how we laughed at how dumb the dream would serve.

I pushed past the idea of her leaving this world by joking some more but I had the same thoughts of her destiny--- maybe this will be her last birthday. She was so blunt about her thoughts of being gone. Nothing wrong, since I preferred to know her true feelings vice later finding she was pretending to be ok.

It was not long before her comments would have a sound of hopelessness. She felt as though God had intended her life to be fast paced. She had compared her choices of living to that of some people who had attempted to take their own lives but lived. Here I was listening to her feeling like her life was marked as "too short".

While growing up she was the one who took on the mother role. She was always there when mom could not. Most importantly she was holding the family together when no one else attempted to. So by knowing that all my life she had held me by the hand I was devastated to feel I couldn't hold hers.

I felt terrible knowing that even when she brought God into her understanding that it always concluded with her time being cut short. I have to admit, her health issues continued to expand into more serious causes. Even worst was knowing that while her medical expenses grew her financial means suffered.

It was apparent that she was "sick and tired" of trying so hard to only be set back by limitations. In the first few years of my military career I made attempts at assisting her financially but in no time even I was struggling to help her. How I hated knowing she was suffering more than we were.

I would listen as she would comment on how she just wanted her son to grow old enough before she is gone. She kept a level of faith but just imagine the life she had to endure. Here she was once a young teenager coping with the responsibilities of an adult. By the age of 17 she was forced out of her education by having to find a means to care for siblings and now her child.

By her mid 20's she had many health problems prolonging her opportunities for education. Eventually giving up was all she could do. So instead of feeling like a successful woman she had to bargain with feeling like a failure. Though this was her thoughts she still put forth words of wisdom to push the rest of us for a better outcome.

Not once did she ever look down at us and make us feel less than perfect. She was always the first one to congratulate the family and the last one to pass judgment of jealousy. Through her sickness she still continued her loving ways towards us. It was as though she didn't see us as her siblings. Instead we were her children.

Fact was that we actually always treated her like our second mother. Because of that it became difficult to feel like I couldn't give back to her the life she ensured I needed. I wanted to be sick for her, I wanted to be tired physically for her, I wanted to feel her soreness spiritually for her, but I could not.

Soon it was time for me to lean on her for some comfort. I had begun to feel sick for awhile. I had made several attempts to see a doctor and find the problem but it always came to no solid conclusion. Instead they were treating symptoms because it seemed like all the test came out normal. Finally, out of the blue, the doctor had made a call to my work place during my absence and asked that I return his call.

Three days later I returned the call and while on the phone he repeats my symptoms. It went from a common review of a possible condition to narrowing down the cause. From the doctor's perspective, all I needed was a minor surgery.
Not necessarily the worst news considering there were no worries in the doctors voice.

I was a bit upset at how long it took for the observation to be completed considering the pain I was in. But within a few days I kind of settle my thoughts on just being grateful for the call. To be unhappy in one matter of life and satisfied in another would be selfish. I know that the nature of the unknown falls with God and not man.

Even more, I was glad for the care and concern I received from my sister. Through this my sister only said positive things to me. She would also keep me informed of my children so that I could keep my sanity that came from missing them. She still did not fail to look past her own sickness to reach out to me and care lovingly. It was amazing how she was looking past her own pain unselfishly to attend to mine.

At this point I was still awaiting my surgery but while I passed the information to my (ex-husband) now fiancé (yes I said it correct) I realized something. My sister had stood by me through such a simple health problem that would be fixed in no time while her very body ached in pain daily. Her pain was not going away and no medication could improve her condition.

She had undoubtedly reminded me that even when our physical body is far from recovery our hearts can remain healthy. No matter how "sick and tired" we may become our strength comes from our actions. I'm sure she woke up that morning in the worst pain imaginable. She possibly stopped a few times along her way to catch her breath while placing a hand over some chest pains.

I do not doubt that when she felt tired her faith and courage kept her moving. When she could have cursed God she only asked that she be allowed her "good-bye". I know I will recover from this primarily because even if my body remains "sick and tired" God will give me rest. She thought me that knowing God is not about wanting for oneself but doing for others. To just set aside your own pain to assist someone else who may not know how to cope with theirs.

All these years and she still had not failed me. Look around, there is always someone else who are at their worst physically but yet has reached out to more lives. Even through those aches and pains she endures daily she was still willing to take another painful step. She still did everything to show me that she was a support system. Not once did she complain about her own pain as she tried to ensure me that I was as healthy as my very soul (Thank you Sis').

CHAPTER FIFTEEN: PUT TO REST

I was finally recovering from my surgery shortly after two weeks. Though I was still slow paced in my walk I still attended church almost immediately. I was maintaining my strict dedication especially now. A lot of the inspiration came from feeling like I was really at home in this church family.

It's such an awesome feeling. To know that you can be surrounded by a variety of individuals and still have a common factor. I especially liked that songs came from anywhere in the room. It wasn't a billet for the choir to control. If in any instance you wanted to praise in your song of liking you could and others would follow.

I went from hiding somewhere in the back of the crowd to slowly moving towards the front. In a figure of speech, I was moving ahead. I was finally tearing down some of my barriers. The ones I once thought were a sign of weakness.

I couldn't explain why I felt this way with this church. This was a new feeling to me. I can recall, during my transformation phase, when I really did not feel like part of "...a church family". Of Course, during that time I was attending a different church. It just felt like a lot of the focus was more on where I had come from.

In fact I can clearly remember once being asked at the previous church "What religion where you raised in?" My reply was simple and I explained how even with the background I never really believed in a "God" growing up. That conversation ended with being told that I basically needed to rebuild myself. As not to destroy (or allow room for evil) to conquer the ways of my husband. Nothing more was considered of my presence. I was merely a third wheel with no name.

It had been my very first meeting at the church so therefore I didn't say anything else. My immediately impression was that my clothes and my background were not wanted there. I felt terrible because my husband (at the time) was trying to share this part of his life---GOD. Also, because it was an answer that further expressed how unprepared my family (growing up) was for faith (as I had decipher the meaning to be). Therefore I felt like I needed to keep distant.

It had been a year since then and I realized that regardless of the conclusion of that conversation, God loved me just as I am. Most importantly, that we are all equal in God's eyes. I had once wondered how I was going to find the right church. Well it didn't take long because instead of looking for a specific religion I had decided to just look for God himself.

I didn't know how to pray at the time but I made the best attempt. I simply asked God to please send me where he wanted me. To bring me to the church where I could feel at home. You know what happened next? Let me explain, less than two days later I had dreamed of being in a church. I was in there joyful as can be. In the dream I actually felt stressed free.

I remember looking around in the dream and saw primarily elderly believers. I was holding hands at the altar with the church and realized that though we didn't fit in this small building we had made the best of it. I couldn't see the pastor's face but I could tell he was of light complexion. I can't remember the rest but I immediately knew that it was my answer. How to find the church was another thing.

Not long after I was driving to a medical appointment at a Naval Hospital in the town I lived and for the first time I had drove by this small church and was immediately drawn. It took about a month before I actually attended. Primarily because I was afraid to be a first time guest since it required introduction. Eventually I was invited by a co-worker and thus had gathered the strength to attend and from that point on I felt a difference.

My first day was served with nothing but hugs and the only question from anyone was "What's your name?" There was a choir and a few musicians but that didn't stop this small church from singing together on their feet. For its small church size it was filled with lots of praise. Almost immediately I recalled scenes of my dream. It had broken me down to my soft sentiments. I was glad for this.

By the end of the day I was approached by a member of the church. She was kindly showing appreciation for my attendance. It was then that I said to her "I've been here before". She then said something to the nature of not remembering my face. It was then that I said "No, I was here in a dream...I had dreamed I had come here. It's the exact layout I saw in it".

She didn't look at me strange (or like I was crazy) as I had assumed considering we were strangers to one another. Especially with the statement I had just related. Instead she nodded and said "God works mysteriously". I had smiled, hugged her, and left. It was on that day I knew for a fact that God found my family. He had a place I could go to praise joyfully.

I was especially glad that God had taken me from such a confused state of mind and brought me closure. I needed to find a church where I could feel like part of the family. I no longer wanted to hide behind the crowd because I had felt less than them.

I am not implying that the previous church is not of God but that it was not for me. It was important to know that although I did not blossom in the last church that it didn't mean I wasn't a blossom at all. Just meant I would have to look for my own place. With God's help I did.

CHAPTER SIXTEEN: BLOOM WHERE YOU ARE PLANTED

Change is gradual and in order to maintain them we must be consistent. I know the journey will be long and it will be difficult but it will also be rewarding in the end. Why continue procrastinating on decisions that will only assist in building us as a whole! He is not far from reach, all we have to do is pray and he will answer.

Many times we fall quickly victims to our environment and thus rely on judgment and excuses. We only grow stronger in hate in this manner. I can personally understand the hardship with trying to find faith in the dark. There had been times when I depended on what I could immediately see in order to believe.....well believe and you will see. Our eyes only see those things when there is light but how are we to be guided with our own eyes when we sit in darkness?....believe in him who guides us and you will see clearly with faith.

There are choices we make and they are not always verbally. Our actions are like seeds planted in our souls. Imagine growing a rose garden and even with the greatest nourishment you find that weeds grow nearby ready to multiply and conquer. Flowers grow in stems and batches but weeds grow in vines. If you pull one from its root you'll find that many more sit on the same vine. They grow in this manner to expedite low resistance in other plants growing in the same field.

Not only are we responsible for the seed that we plant but what seed we are planting. Reflecting back to my childhood days I can recall a moment when I had stopped talking to one of my brothers. It wasn't rare for one of us to stop speaking to another but this had been my first time making that decision for myself. We had grown in hate over a small bitter fight. Over the course of weeks I continued to purposely say hateful things. At the time I was venting my anger toward the situation.

I remember walking down the school halls with my books in hand and he would walk past me and I would just look the other way. His stare was that of an apologetic stand point. Eventually I gave in to speaking to him again but neither of us ever apologized. We were at home one day and I had responded to a question he had asked another sibling. From that point on we were back on speaking terms. In the aftermath I realized how much time was consumed with building hatred.

Regardless of opinion no excuse served enough evidence against being ignorant. We had turned the soil dry and allowed time for weeds to grow in our once blossomed flower bed. It was time to "weed-out" the negativity. Once the dust had settled we took a more realistic approach and planted new hope. We began to go back to our joking ways and rebuild the bond.

I was glad for this. He was my brother, one of few who I had spent nearly every growing experience with. He was funny by nature but most importantly I had admired his way in keeping a smile on my mom's face. I could recall how my youngest brother and I would get our fair punishments....oh but not him; he would break all the rules but find the most hilarious form of explaining his reasoning. This would eventually lead to her bursting into laughter and surpassing his punishment.

Now that we are much older it's pretty funny to picture his technique. I could always tell he did so to keep the air at home clear. I'm sure this took a lot of effort to enhance. He, somehow, managed to bloom a sight of joy in my mom who always wore the look of exhaustion. He planted that seed and it blossomed well.

I could only imagine how we affect God's field. We have become like a band of weeds seeking to overturn the ground beneath our very own feet for self satisfaction. I cannot count the many times that I've looked out into my own yard and seen the turmoil. Watching my seeds drown with hopelessness and depression. Of course it usually seems easier to stop planting our seeds to avoid noticing our impact.

Fact is the "...grass is greener on the other side"....because we prefer to compliment someone else on their hard work oppose to enhancing our "green thumb". I was starring off into the neighbor's yard watching their plants grow healthy with joy. It was proof of the impossible and yet my sowed seed had gone dry. It took realizing that when it storms and rains God still provides our basic essentials for growth.

He was ensuring that I was not lacking any potential but before anything could blossom it was my job to ensure I was planting my seed. My task was obvious, before I could put any further burdens in God's hands; I needed to ensure my feet were planted on solid ground. Avoiding discipline in my ways would only serve disaster. Therefore I sought a narrowed path in God's will.

This brings me back to a favorite cadence song I've learned during my military career that says...."Don't let the green grass fool you", Don't let it change your mind". It's important to take care of our home front first and avoid trying to move on to another field to only poison that soil also.

We cannot grow roses in our flower bed solely on sun rays alone. We have sorrows that will come along the way. Getting lost in the storm is easier than finding hope...but I know with God nothing is impossible. We can remove stones by prayer and cast blessings from our seeds. The best part of a fruitful seed is its flavorful taste. It all starts with planting our seeds and blooming where you're planted.

This is where our labor pays off. Even when we become tired physically or spiritually he will provide according to our hard work. I am preparing my seed to be planted in great soil where it will reproduce high quality. The question is: Are you planting your seed for a lifetime or will it be seasonal?

CHAPTER SEVENTEEN: LOST CAUSE

He isn't through with me yet. God still had many more "teacher-scholar" lessons to push my way. The blessings continued to flow. The best feeling is to know that above blessing me as an individual he still provided me the strength to reach out others. To become an inspiration or that shoulder that lightens up burdens. When I speak of God to anyone I can hear them take a sigh. A relief that says "Thank you God for all you do...."

Even after an unpredictable childhood, confusing young adulthood, and a reality into family bond, he has placed me as a winning trophy. I wasn't a gold medalist or even a bronze medalist but I became a loved child of God. I had ran many miles and though I didn't think I could finish the race he inspired the way.

When he found me lost in the woods, though everyone else had given up hope of my survival, he had also found my lost dreams. He fulfilled every part of my life that once held on by sorrows. Look at me today, I still continue to feel the rain but in it I sing with joy and dance in the storm. To him I will never be a LOST CAUSE.

Can you imagine how it feels to have seen the foundation beneath your feet fall apart? To laugh on the outside but burn in pain on the inside?. The world will always be eyes on the outside looking in....but God he sees the pain in our hearts.

I can count years of knowing that I was just an image. Part of a portrait that was hung in silence. When my family lacked in God we had also lacked in opportunity. We had closed those doors that can only unlock with faith and forgiveness. Today....yes today....we have one another. The dust was wiped from the portrait, this time with love.

Have you ever read a "Lost and Found" classified? It usually begins with a description of the item lost and is then followed by the location where it was found. In most cases the condition of the item is also described. The post only serves as hope that someone will claim their lost item. It's obvious that the founder has every desire of reaching the owner so that the item of great significance be returned. Maybe Grandpa's old watch or Momma's favorite ring.

The owner is usually aware that he/she has lost something possibly irreplaceable. Of course not aware that his/her lost history has been found and awaiting claim. Chances are they have started to move on with a piece of them missing. This is not necessarily how they would like to carry on but instead of hope they exercise adaptation.

The founder still continues to pursue a satisfying claim. At this point probably wondering about what more could be done to track the owner. Yet advertisement continues for weeks unending and finally the owner happens to pick up a newspaper at the store and begins to read the latest and most current event. After reading the most popular part of the paper he/she sees no further purpose in reading on but continues.

In no time the owner reaches the back of the newspaper and finds the classified ad and finally......he/she is amazed and grateful to have found that significant item that had became hopeless to find. With excitement the owner calls and finds that all the time he/she stopped looking the founder was still hopeful. Now what was once LOST without a trace has been FOUND.

Now think of us as a lost soul trying to find our place. Moving on with our lives not knowing where we belong. All the while God stands confidently seeking your return back to the path you steered away from. There you are carrying on but not whole, just torn in two. Your doubts beginning to cloud the very existence of God.

You reach a moment of believing deep down that nothing is possible at this point to include the grace of God. Yet he continues to publish your path by opening ways to communicate his will for you. You had left behind a part of you that now seems far from reach, the part of you that seeks God. You figure that you can cope with this loss now that all signs point to popular demand of just forgetting.

Days pass, weeks end, even months change....yet still no hope. Convinced by what has not occurred in your favor you begin to change your priorities. Seeking the spotlight that only serves as today's hot topic and tomorrow's forgotten news. You put ahead things and ideals while finding no interest in reading behind the popular story. Finally you find the courage to read between the lines. In the process you find that while you had carried on with a part of yourself missing he was waiting patiently to restore you whole.

Gratefully you make the life changing call and he answers. Though your voice once spoke doubts, the voice on the other end gracefully responds to you. You now have that meaningful, once lost, missing part of you back. You begin to feel complete and counting the odds knowing that it couldn't have been possible. All this time had passed and you had once grown tired. Now thinking back you realize that in God you were no lost cause.

I tell you, this is how I feel about God's love. If I lose sight a thousand times he would have already searched a thousand and one times for me. He will always be a step ahead of us. Even when our soul becomes lost in the ways of this world with priorities set on disaster he will not stop looking. It just takes calling him to realize that in the midst of doubt you had only been seconds from being FOUND!

CHAPTER EIGHTEEN: STILL HERE

I had been through some obstacles in my life and I am sure by now you are wondering what more could go wrong?...fact: nothing! God had pulled me through in the hardest times. At one point it felt like the problems would not ceased but they have. I am not implying that problems no longer exist in my life but instead that they are at a minimum with faith in God and his will on my side.

Looking back at my life when God had no purpose and was just a "...poorly executed theory" to satisfy purpose in things for mental satisfaction, I could see that I was leading myself into meaningless goals of hate and discontent. I was walking with my head held down and fighting away the world. Today...Now...At this moment...In the after math...With experience----however best describes beginning a new journey and being reborn, I am whole.

Feeling complete spiritually has been a great feeling and has proven to me that we can live solely on faith. I know that I still have a long journey ahead and that I am not made perfect but once again---I am made WHOLE. I am firm at this point that I will not relapse with doubts of God and his purpose for me. Beyond all of my burdens he has given me the gift of sight and strength to help others pull through.

If he could do this for me 'what could he do for you?'. Let me remind you that this is my story, these words express my experience. This is not advertisement but evidence. I may not have a fancy home and fancy cars with extreme income but I know I am rich in love, laughter, and faith. I have my children, speaking with my mom after many years of silence and seeing the air clear of negativity. Because of him (God) I AM STILL HERE....

He has been one of the wisest accomplishments in my life. Many years ago I was lost even when the sun stood still in my path. I was filled with hate and spoke with anger. Society was my only means for development and my intent mirrored those of "no good" and somehow I was once proud of that. Now look at all I've become, I am not perfect and definitely far from it but in the aftermath God has guarded me with hope. Most importantly he had kept me above sea level and given me forgiveness.

What a great feeling to be forgiven. Ever sit back and think about how much it means to be forgiven for even the worst times that cannot be taken back nor replaced?....well God had did it for me. He had seen my story written and in the end he was still standing right there carrying me on his shoulder. The weight of one person is heavy, imagine carrying the whole world. If God isn't awesome then what more can define him!

I have gone from an "Atheist" to a "Believer" and all with trials and tribulations. I did not take a special course on how to become a believer nor had any privileges in life but yet again "I AM STILL HERE...". I didn't find him by accident because God isn't one to "accidently find a person", instead he sought me and he saw purpose in me. I had gone through so much in my life that at one point I couldn't see my own purpose in being around but he did. He somehow knew that all my suffering would reach calm.

My only hope is that it would reach someone else, even if thousands of miles away. I want God to continue blessing because I know he is willing. I don't have the best of things or a "Picture Perfect" family but I do have a story and this story I will continue to tell. I know for myself and with evidence that God is life and without him life has no meaning beyond material things. I know that I have been recovered.

As I continue to write into these pages I find more evidence of what God has pulled me away from. I was keeping my own feet in the fire through my helplessness. Now I must seek to do for others in God's way. I've thought long and hard of how I would reach many in the way that he reached me. How was I going to give back in three folds? I'm sure you're wondering by now why such a long story....well I realized that helping one person at a time is "good" but I wanted to accomplish "great".

While lying in bed one night something within me just took hold and so I grabbed my laptop and I began to write. At the moment I thought that I would only consume one page. In less than five hours it had became seven pages. Not long after I had completed a chapter. I continued typing my story and the more I wrote the more I realized I needed to tell and now it has become a testimony. Yes that's right, living proof of all God has done for me. I may not know what will come tomorrow but today these pages bare that fruit of evidence.

I can clearly remember many years ago when I would curse God. When things were going smoothly I would talk on behalf of God and be content with saying he was there....JUST THERE. As soon as things weren't as I defined as "Good" then I would curse his existence and how it wasn't fair. Later in life I came to analyze myself more in-depth and realized how ungrateful I had been. God only served a purpose for material things and at fault when it wasn't to my means. How could I have been so naive!

As I mentioned earlier, God was "Just there"....he was a factor at times and a common denominator when things went wrong. I was pushing the pull with God. How could I expect to see all his blessings when I had once sought him for material satisfactions. What about the intangibles? What about that opportunity of becoming a mother, that ability to feel love, the chance to wake in the morning and rest at night, what....what....what...

The list goes on and so do I. I am able to move on, this time with love filling my heart. God was "Just there", nothing more. I had not given him the praise and worship that best suited his ways. When we consider anything or anyone "Just there" then it can be easily set aside. It is much like the saying, "Out of sight, Out of mind". Through it I came to realize that even when he knew I considered him the path to point my finger or another ideal of "Just there"....he kept me in his care, stood by me, carried me through many obstacles and yet through it all and because of him I am "Still here".

CHAPTER NINETEEN: A FAMILY THAT PRAYS TOGETHER

My spiritual evolution has provided me with a great tool---Prayer. I have to say that prayer has helped me through many situations. When I need to ease my thoughts I lean on prayer. My favorite one is the Serenity Prayer…

" God, grant me the serenity to accept the things I cannot change, Courage to change the things I can, and Wisdom to know the difference "

This prayer helps me understand that not all will be perfect. In such a short phase it gives me the mental courage to see a positive connection between obstacles. I remember reciting the prayer often a few months after my surgery. Right when I thought I was in my recovery phase everything took an immediate turn in the opposite direction.

My scars were healed and the pain was subsiding. It was later that I went for a routine check-up to allow the doctor to evaluate the healing process. I left my appointment carrying on with my normal daily routine. Well to my surprise the doctor had called me back and related the news that I may have cancer.

The news did not immediately register in my thoughts. It took about two days for me to feel concerned about the situation. I made further plans to have another evaluation and during those conversations I kept hearing---"Don't worry it may be early signs." It was a sound of a possibility in which my doctor relied on scientific facts to support.

When reality finally hit me I was left with finding a reliable source of my own---God. I prayed in hopes that, whatever the outcome of the results, I receive my diagnosis in a timely manner. It would be a matter of weeks before anyone would have the final results. But I wanted to make sure not to waste time that could be utilized in preparing my children's future.

I was a bit scared and confused at the same time. Wait a minute! Just three months ago my health was well. I had my surgery and nothing more came of it, except recovery. So I carried on like my days were marked on "tomorrow". When I think of cancer I am brought to the idea of death. I know people have overcome the odds but at this time I just felt like statistics couldn't ease my sorrow.

I suddenly started preparing a list for videos and letters I would make for my family. To prepare for those occasions in the future where I would not (possibly) be around to enjoy with them. I didn't tell anyone (during this time) to avoid questions that I still had no answers to. Plus it was still just a possibility of a situation. One that reminded me to count my blessings opposed to counting my days.

This was something that at my children's young age I couldn't find the simplest words to explain. My thoughts flooded with finding a mechanism to assist them in coping (if the test resulted in a serious issue of course). Maybe I was overreacting but now I didn't know what sort of plan to execute. Do I prepare a tomorrow for my kids with me or without me?

It was a rare feeling to suddenly acknowledge that life is not a "right". A day before that call I had focused on plans for "tomorrow". I wasn't thinking about the "If's or

Buts" nor consequences. I didn't focus much on the small factors of living. But now I started to question whether or not I had used every second of my completed days wisely.

While my doctor sought his answer through medical research I prayed for one. I am sure that my doctor was hoping for an answer that could ease my worries. But I just wanted a simple answer that would tell me how to commence my planning. I wanted to ensure that all avenues would conclude in happiness.

If described by the body, happiness would be to live and have the best of things (as you pleased). Rather I wanted happiness felt by the heart and soul. The one that see's the good in any perspective. The kind of happiness that informs me, that whatever the results, God had my family in his care. That he would allow me a spare moment to leave my mark for them.

I prayed often asking God to tell me his will for me. I wasn't asking for a specific test result, I didn't ask "Why me?" I just simply wanted him to expose his plans for me. I wanted God to allow me a head start so that I could leave memories for my family to embrace. My desire was on giving them those "last moments" for them to look back on with a smile and not sorrow.

I found myself thinking a lot about the possible results and then realized that science will only be able to give me a diagnosis. It will assume the task to aid in my care. But one thing it couldn't give me was a clear conscience and an accepting heart. It had been through prayers where I truly found a sense of calmness and love that kept me focused. It was very helpful to have that soul healing. I became confident that I was going to be at home---regardless.

Look at how we want answers on how to live our lives! A measurement imposed on our desires. We shift our focus on the physical until life fails to provide those selfish satisfactions. I am as guilty as anyone else in this sense. Sadly I had to be faced with such a problem to understand it for myself.

I guess in the same idea I can accept that science is right about one thing....it's mind over matter. In a sort of funny way, the only things that matter are beyond the physical limitations. We easily proclaim life in relation to what we have, well after this rude awakening I see it differently now. Life is......living in appreciation---that should be the main foundation to our individual desires. The factors that keep us functioning in the right state of MIND.

In a broader insight, when materials things fail us it's then that we are drawn to seeking God. Ever wonder why that is? I am convinced that it's due to our conscious mind telling us that something much greater than society's way of life exist. I've try to hypothesize my life but fact stands that I won't have answers to my own conclusion. God is ultimately the key player in all aspects of life---he is in fact the beginning and the end.

Fairly, with such a situation I wouldn't want that detail knowledge. It is not having knowledge of those fine details that allows us room to smile. I guess this is why I don't characterize God as a problem anymore. Cancer or not, I wouldn't want to carry the burden of knowing when time would cease to ring in my ear.

I went to church after finding out about my cancer prognosis and I walked up to the altar. The church prayed for me although I did not provide information for needing prayer. I just walked up and lowered my head as thoughts, both positive and negative, clouded me. As I listened it felt like they were aware of my situation.

It was as though my thoughts were written for all to see. I do not know what more to say of this experience except that I felt confident that all was well. If by this odd chance they could feel my pain then I knew God was bringing them knowledge. He was planting them rightfully in my path so that I would at least know that he was aware of my fear.

God was ensuring my peace of mind. With only a few spoken words of prayer from the church I felt my worries fall off my shoulders. I left the church glad to have my biological and church family available. I was reminded that they were all "PERFECT" in my life. Nothing was wrong with my family because, for as long as we are praying for one another, we will always be by each other's side.

All those years I had thought we didn't carry one another dearly. Moments where I had assume we had refused to reach over and provide comfort. Right when they couldn't stand next to me physically they appeared spiritually. The chain that I once thought was stretched too far from recovery had been broken. It was soon replaced with prayer and the gap mended.

In much appreciation, my family and I had struggle together, felt the loneliness together, and eventually came together. Somehow without notice we had gone through all our difficult phases as a family. At the time we didn't realize it because we thought the situations were just unique to ourselves but looking back…we were making it through as a FAMILY.

All I can further say is; if doubts of the power of prayer still keep you leaning on coincidence then it is time to stop reading beyond this point. By some odd factor you might just witness that COINCIDENCE has a powerful name. A name that produces quality without regards to human faults. One that has given me the days of life to finish strong.

CHAPTER TWENTY: A GOD LOVING ATHEIST

The anticipated call came through to give an end to my worries. I listened calmly but my thoughts were impatiently trying to speed up time. The nurse on the other end of the phone finally stated "The test proved the abnormal cells". She continued with further information about the diagnosis.

She briefly explained the stages of growth cancer cells go through and my results in relation to the possibilities. I was actually at work when I received the call so I made every effort not to cry. I was really thankful that I would only have to do early stage treatment for preventive measures. I couldn't have asked for better.

My fear was only a portion of the worry. Having gone through this brought me back to my own childhood where I didn't have a father around. The environment that secluded me into the world society portrayed on popular demand. I was once very confused trying to understand, on what I thought, were unjust sufferings.

Strangely my biological father died of cancer when I was only four years old. When problems became constant in my family I always wondered what would be different if he was still alive. Especially since I was able to see how it was like not having him around. I was just a child with no father so it was only by thoughts that I tried to fill the void.

During that time in my life I just couldn't put meaning into my environment. I once actually wondered that if God was writing my story why then would he write it with so much hate and sorrows. I was sure that people only desired that "Happily Ever After" ending. A story that portrays us as the hero.

Obviously, those were the factors that made me proclaim myself an ATHEIST. I was firm that there could be no God if I am suppose to be thankful for sorrows. Why? Why should I have to show God that I can love him at my worst? I rationalized my ideals to the point of thinking that I was outsmarting the existence of God.

Of course, in my mind it all had to be a matter of common sense. That if "God is the way" that there should be no need for me to have to prove myself to see the way. Ultimately God became a poorly proven hypothesis. I was even convinced that someone, many centuries ago, forgot to consider reality during the testing phase. Thus concluding with what would be considered as "supernatural".

Therefore I found it best to deny the belief. In my own belief, God was merely an excuse to find a mental way through problems without having to face them physically. God was Santa Clause with the exception of reindeers. Both of which were great fables.

Well I could not have been so right. To have not believed and denying the existence of God was the best thing I've ever done for myself. To have carried myself accordingly, as an ATHEIST, with persuasive logical explanations of those so called "blessings". I had vividly experienced a world without God while still finding no correlation to all aspects of life.

Indeed, denying God was a step well taken because in the end it had been what brought me to finding God. It was a matter of adding all that the human eye could see and calculating it to all that had been accomplished in my life. Eventually finding out that nothing could have been possible without a higher power. Amazingly, being a believer all of your life isn't the only way to finding God.

The only thing I had to do, to find out if God exist, was to look back at my trials. I tell you, when I attempted to explain the outcome of many gray areas in my life I couldn't find an excuse. Nor that scientific evidence to solidify, on all accounts, God's lacking role. I am convinced that I only made it this far with the grace of God.

The absolute turning point for me was during my first Marriage. My husband and I had moved in together in a small two bedroom house. The house was probably more than 20 years old. It wasn't in bad shape but the appliances definitely showed its age.

About two days before Christmas Eve of 2006 I had started to feel a bit sick. I had spent the entire day at work nearly with no energy. By the time I got home the only thing I could do was lay down to sleep. My husband took care of the chores that day.

Somewhere between midnight and one o'clock in the morning I began to smell smoke. Still tired I shouted to my husband asking him to turn off the stove. He replied and assured me the stove was off. Within a few minutes the smoke felt thick and I awoke again to a slight cloud on the ceiling.

This time I yelled at my husband angrily to turn the stove off. I wasn't sure why I kept saying the stove was the cause of the smoke but it was in my conscious to say. My husband replied again, while lying next to me in the bed that the stove was not on. I was startled a bit and continued with asking him to get up and check the stove.

Once again, he checks and tells me not to be concerned. In no time this strong odor has me sort of irritated and I felt like a strong smell was overcoming my senses. I was convinced that a smoky-like odor filled our room. My constant concern eventually led to us arguing. Due to the argument we never went back to sleep and we headed to work early.

We both left the house with unspoken words. Three hours later, about nine in the morning he calls me. To my shock, he called to inform me that "The neighbor called to say that our house is on fire". I immediately started my car and hurried to the house.

By the time I arrive to the house the fire department, my husband, and my command were there. I couldn't believe that we were losing everything just days before Christmas and less than a month before my one year deployment. My husband walks over to me and holds me as we watch our house burn. All I could do was to stand there holding back tears.

Once the fire department managed to settle the fire a detective approaches us. He starts with "Do you have renter's insurance?" and we reply with "No". He then explains that the house was obviously old and that the stove was a gas stove. He continues with saying that the gas tank underneath the house apparently had a leak.

With our bedroom only being a wall away from the kitchen our bed was completely burned. The scariest part was that the only areas the explosion affected were the kitchen, the small bathroom near the room and our bedroom. Those specific areas were now mostly unrecognizable.

Just looking around the house broke my heart. All I could think about is "Why now? Why did this happen now? How are we going to get back on our feet?" We managed to salvage plenty of items especially those things in the living room not damaged by the smoke.

After we managed to move some items we stayed at my brother-in-laws house and it was there that my husband mentioned what he considered "A sign from God". He explained that somehow I had become the messenger in this sign. I was really stressed out at the moment so I just asked him to stop putting God where he wasn't fit for recognition.

A few years had passed and I could remember that night like it was just yesterday. Looking back at it now, God was on my side. I truly understand what people mean when they say "God told me..." because I also felt like something was giving me information. I never once got up from the bed because I felt sick and yet something pointed out the stove.

I would have passed that experience as a coincidence but somehow I do not believe coincidence has a voice that speaks to one's conscious. I tell you, I am still standing with minor scars where there should have been permanent disfiguring in my life. I was definitely shielded with the highest quality of love.

To exemplify to the proper level the impact God had, I must ask "How then did I get here?" Pieces of what I thought were a broken environment had come together like pieces to a puzzle. When I look at this picture I can see God standing where I had once thought I had been alone.

I know now that God's love is unconditional and that he in fact loved me at my worst. Those obstacles that once made me refuse God now serve as evidence. It was those moments of sorrow that became the foundation of the plan God had in place for me. God wrote my story so beautifully. "…and she lived **HAPPILY EVER AFTER— ALL**".

Having been an atheist by definition gave me the opportunity to witness for myself the existence of God. It was like God had actually taken up the fight to prove me wrong when I had placed a blindfold over faith. I have decided to remind myself of that long journey by strongly refusing to change the definition of my true self. I will continue to acknowledge that I was once a non-believer. I am in fact an Atheist turned Believer. This is why I now proclaim myself

"A GOD LOVING *ATHEIST*"

A GOD LOVING

ATHEIST